BUILD UP YOUR
LEGO WINTER VILLAGE

by David Younger

CHRISTMAS TRAIN

www.inklingbricks.com

Introduction

Since 2009, The LEGO Group has made getting a new Winter Village set an annual tradition — but with just one Winter Village set being released each year, the desire to grow your village can quickly outpace the available sets! This book is a solution to that.

Within these pages you'll find brand new models you can use to grow your Winter Village. Simply search through your Lego tubs, order the pieces you're missing, then get building up your very own winter wonderland.

Official sets	
2009	**10199** Winter Toy Shop
2010	**10216** Winter Village Bakery
2011	**10222** Winter Village Post Office
2012	**10229** Winter Village Cottage
2013	**10235** Winter Village Market
2014	**10245** Santa's Workshop
2015	**10249** Winter Toy Shop (Rerelease)
2016	**10254** Winter Holiday Train
2017	**10259** Winter Village Station
2018	**10263** Winter Village Fire Station
2019	**10267** Gingerbread House
2020	**10275** Elf Club House

Contents

How to get the bricks

Most people's first step for getting all the needed bricks will be their own collection of LEGO bricks! Use the brick lists at the end of each set instructions to find the bricks you already have, and figure out what you still need to get. It's easy to order any bricks you still need.

LEGO.com

Aside from the Pick a Brick walls at the official LEGO Stores, there are two ways LEGO allows you to purchase individual LEGO bricks through their website at **www.LEGO.com**: Pick A Brick and Bricks & Pieces (to find this, click Support then Replacement Parts).

For both services, you can simply type in the part number (shown in the Brick List for each model) to search for it. Please note that LEGO.com's part availability constantly changes depending on which LEGO bricks are being manufactured at the time so not everything might be available.

Bricklink

www.Bricklink.com is a website owned and operated by The LEGO Group which brings together numerous independent sellers from around the world who all run their own stores selling individual LEGO bricks. Buyers can shop for bricks individually, or upload Wanted Lists and use Bricklink's auto-finder to generate a list of stores that you can buy from to get all the bricks you need. You also have the option of buying brand new or used.

Uploading a Wanted List

Rather than having to add every brick to a wanted list individually, Bricklink allows you to upload lists of bricks to generate an entire wanted list in one go. The list for each model can be found at the web address at the beginning of each model's section in this book. Head to that address and then follow these steps:

1. Select all the text and copy it. It should begin with <INVENTORY> and end with </INVENTORY>.

2. Sign into Bricklink.com, hover over Want at the top right, then click Upload.

3. Click Upload BrickLink XML format.

4. In the drop down box next to Add to select Create New Wanted List and type in a name for your new wanted list a name.

5. Right click in the box which says Copy and paste here and click paste to paste in the XML code.

6. Click Proceeed to verify items and then Add to Wanted List at the bottom of the next page.

Your wanted list is now uploaded! Hover over Want at the top right of Bricklink then click Wanted List to see a all of your wanted lists.

Buying bricks with Bricklink

Although you can buy bricks individually, the quickest way to do this is with Bricklink's auto-finder feature:

1. From the Wanted List page, click the name of the Wanted List you'd like to purchase, then click the Buy All button.

2. Set the locations you're willing to purchase from with the Store Location drop down buttons.

3. Click the Auto-select button and then Start. This will create a list of stores that combined have all your needed bricks assigned to it.

4. Check the assigned percentage at the top right. If this is below 100%, some bricks can't be found from the stores specified in your search preferences. You may need to widen the stores you're willing to buy from, search for a used part instead of a new part, or substitute it. To find out which bricks these are, scroll down below the list, and click Wanted Items.

5. If everything looks good, however, click Create carts to add them to your cart, then click Checkout one by one from each store to purchase the bricks you need from each individual seller.

It's very rare that a single store will have all the bricks you need, so you should expect to be buying from multiple sellers – just remember that you'll need to pay postage on each separate store order.

How to keep the price low

Because Bricklink doesn't use set prices, the cost of bricks can vary between sellers. Here are some techniques for getting the cost as low as it can go:

Finding the expensive bricks

When you have your list of stores, before you click Create carts, you can click the Edit button beside each store to see which bricks you're buying from them. In the Sort by drop down box, choose Price and then scroll to the bottom to see which bricks are the most expensive.

Substitutions

One of the best things about LEGO is how versatile it is, so it's easy to swap bricks out for others. If a 1x8 brick is too expensive, for example, try swapping it for two 1x4 bricks – but always check the instructions to ensure a brick isn't structurally important first. Or if a specific color is too expensive, try swapping it for a more available color. You can make these changes on the Wanted List page, then simply run the auto-finder again.

Avoiding expensive stores

If a particular store is too expensive overall, you can exclude it from the auto-finder results. Click the store name to go to its store page, click the Favorite Stores drop-down box at the top, click Bookmark this store, then choose Dislike before clicking Bookmark.

The most common substitutions for train pieces are the wheels and the magnetic couplers. Make sure you price all of them up to find out what will be cheapest for you:

Wheels	Couplers
2878c02	29085c01
38339c01	91994

LOCOMOTIVE

Number of bricks: 350

www.inklingbricks.com/parts/locomotive.txt

1

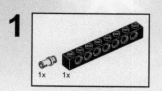

2

3

4

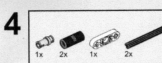

5

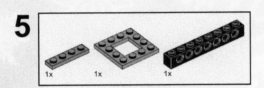

6

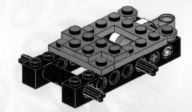

7

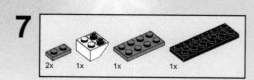

2x 1x 1x 1x

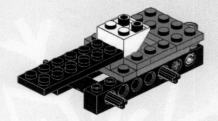

8

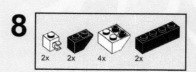

2x 2x 4x 2x

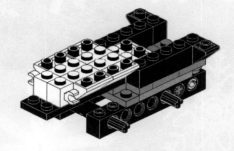

9

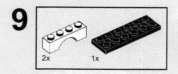

2x 1x

10

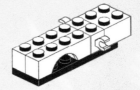

11

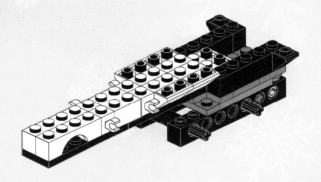

12

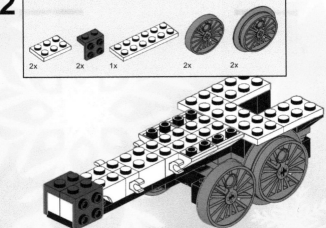

13

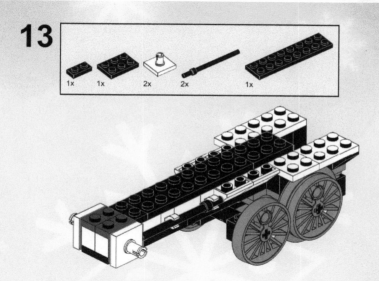

1x 1x 2x 2x 1x

14

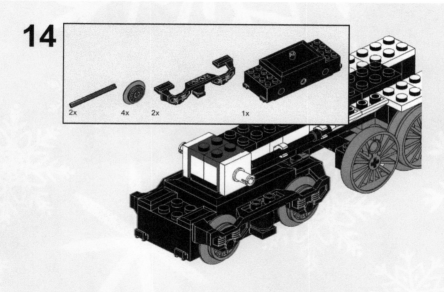

2x 4x 2x 1x

15

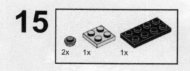

2x 1x 1x

16

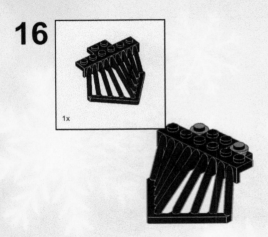

1x

17

2x 1x

18

3x 2x 2x 2x 2x

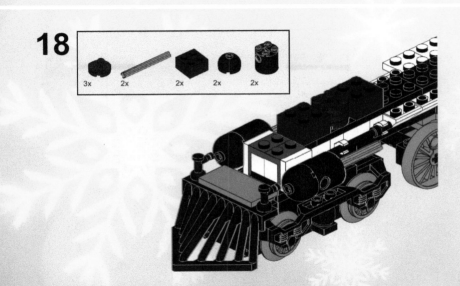

19

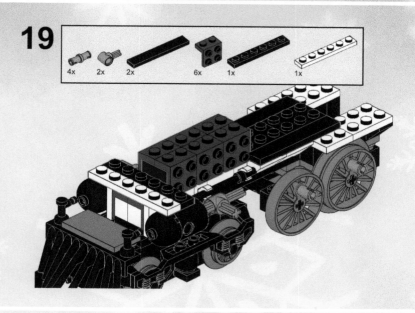

20

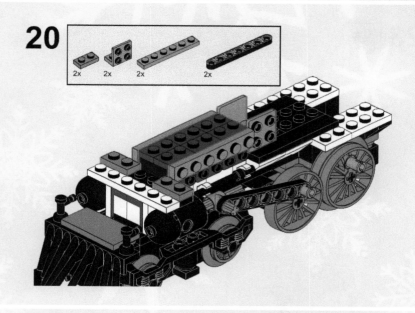

21

22

23

24

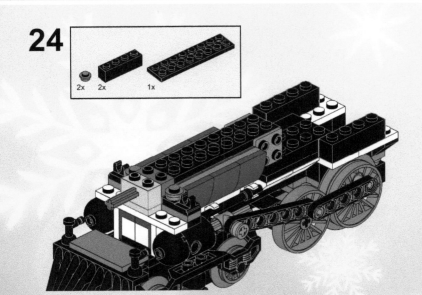

25

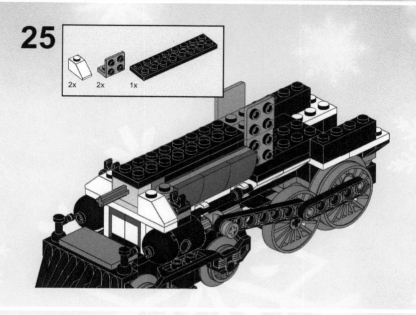

26

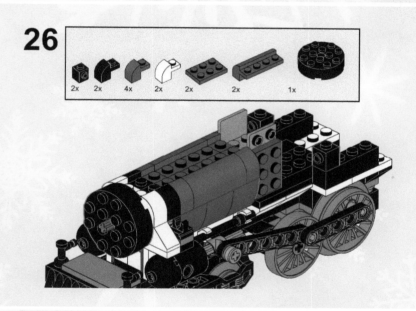

27

28

1x 1x 1x

29

2x 1x 1x

30

1x 3x 1x 1x 1x

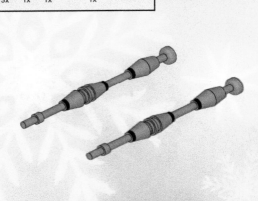

16

31

32

33

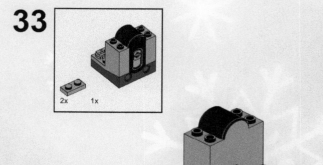

34

35

36

37

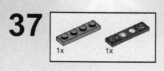
1x   1x

38

39

1x   1x

40

41

42

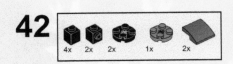

43

2x 4x 1x 2x 4x 1x

44

1x 1x 1x 2x

45

2x 2x 7x 2x 1x 2x 1x

46

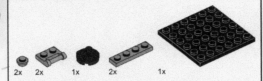

2x 2x 1x 2x 1x

47

1x 2x 4x 2x 1x

48

49

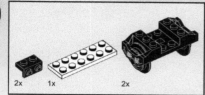

50

51

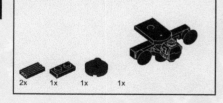

52

4x   1x

53

4x 2x 2x 1x 1x

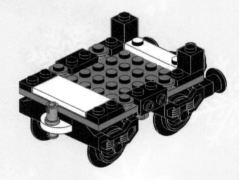

54

2x 2x 6x

55

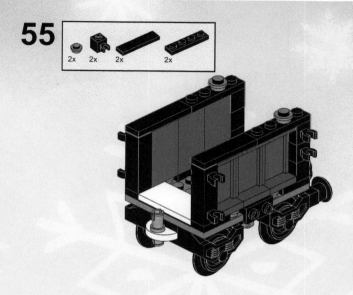

2x 2x 2x 2x

56

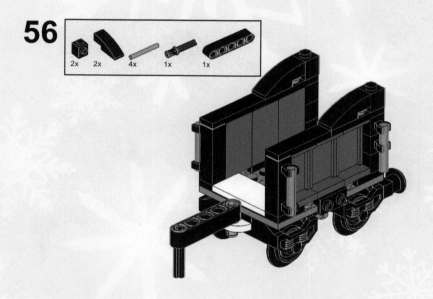

2x 2x 4x 1x 1x

57

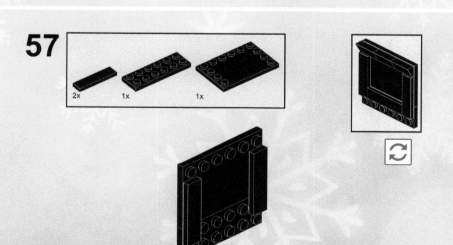

2x 1x 1x

58

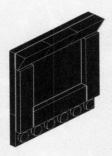

59

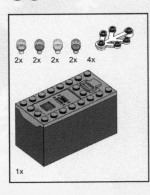

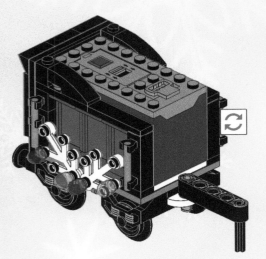

60

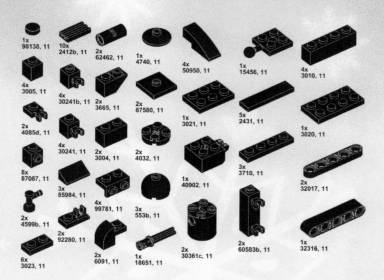

1x 98138, 11
10x 2412b, 11
2x 62462, 11
1x 4740, 11
4x 50950, 11
1x 15456, 11
4x 3010, 11

4x 3005, 11
4x 30241b, 11
2x 3665, 11
2x 87580, 11
1x 3021, 11
5x 2431, 11
1x 3020, 11

2x 4085d, 11
4x 30241, 11
2x 3004, 11
2x 4032, 11
3x 3710, 11
2x 32017, 11

8x 87087, 11
3x 85984, 11
1x 40902, 11

2x 4599b, 11
4x 99781, 11
3x 553b, 11
2x 60583b, 11

2x 92280, 11
2x 30361c, 11
1x 32316, 11

6x 3023, 11
2x 6091, 11
1x 18651, 11

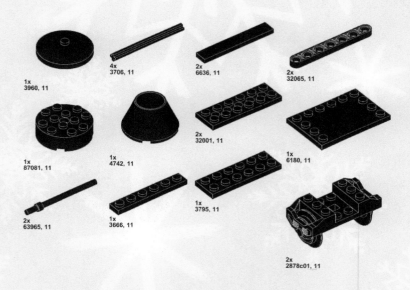

1x 3960, 11
4x 3706, 11
2x 6636, 11
2x 32065, 11

2x 32001, 11

1x 87081, 11
1x 4742, 11
1x 6180, 11

2x 63965, 11
1x 3666, 11
1x 3795, 11

2x 2878c01, 11

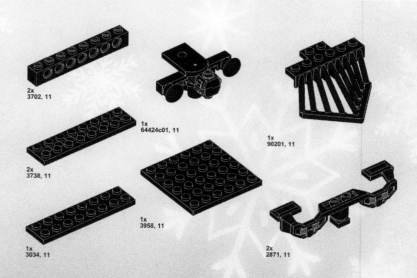

2x 3702, 11
1x 64424c01, 11
1x 90201, 11

2x 3738, 11

1x 3958, 11

1x 3034, 11
2x 2871, 11

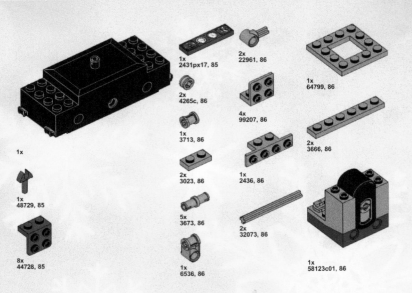

1x

1x
48729, 85

8x
44728, 85

1x
2431px17, 85

2x
22961, 86

2x
4265c, 86

4x
99207, 86

1x
3713, 86

2x
3023, 86

1x
2436, 86

5x
3673, 86

1x
6536, 86

2x
32073, 86

1x
64799, 86

2x
3666, 86

1x
58123c01, 86

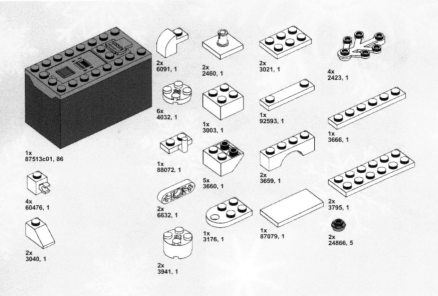

1x
87513c01, 86

4x
60476, 1

2x
3040, 1

2x
6091, 1

6x
4032, 1

1x
88072, 1

2x
6632, 1

2x
3941, 1

2x
2460, 1

1x
3003, 1

5x
3660, 1

1x
3176, 1

2x
3021, 1

1x
92593, 1

2x
3659, 1

1x
87079, 1

4x
2423, 1

1x
3666, 1

2x
3795, 1

2x
24866, 5

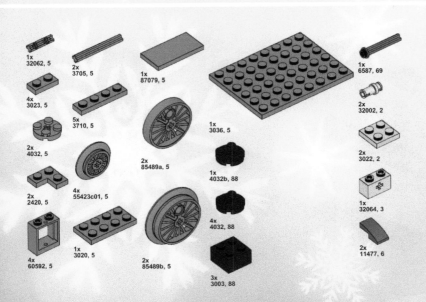

1x
32062, 5

4x
3023, 5

2x
4032, 5

2x
2420, 5

4x
60592, 5

2x
3705, 5

5x
3710, 5

4x
55423c01, 5

1x
3020, 5

1x
87079, 5

2x
85489a, 5

2x
85489b, 5

1x
3036, 5

1x
4032b, 88

4x
4032, 88

3x
3003, 88

1x
6587, 69

2x
32002, 2

2x
3022, 2

1x
32064, 3

2x
11477, 6

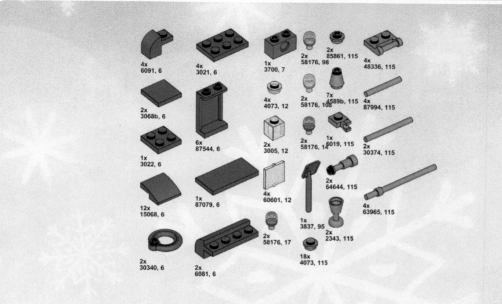

4x
6091, 6

4x
3021, 6

1x
3700, 7

2x
58176, 98

2x
85861, 115

4x
48336, 115

2x
3068b, 6

6x
87544, 6

4x
4073, 12

2x
58176, 108

7x
4589b, 115

4x
87994, 115

1x
3022, 6

2x
3005, 12

2x
58176, 14

1x
6019, 115

2x
30374, 115

12x
15068, 6

1x
87079, 6

4x
60601, 12

2x
64644, 115

4x
63965, 115

2x
30340, 6

2x
6081, 6

2x
58176, 17

1x
3837, 95

2x
2343, 115

18x
4073, 115

PASSENGER CAR

Number of bricks: 250

www.inklingbricks.com/parts/passengercar.txt

1

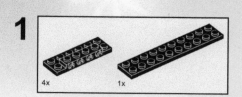

4x   1x

2

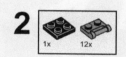

1x   12x

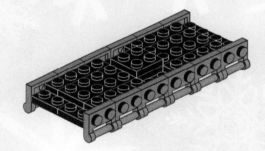

3

4x   2x

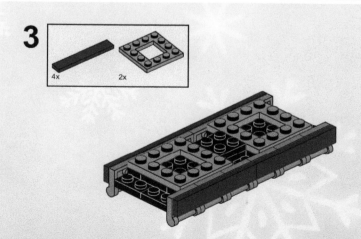

4

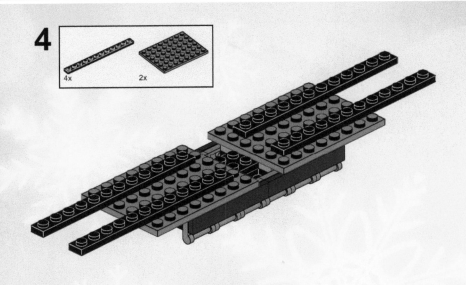

5

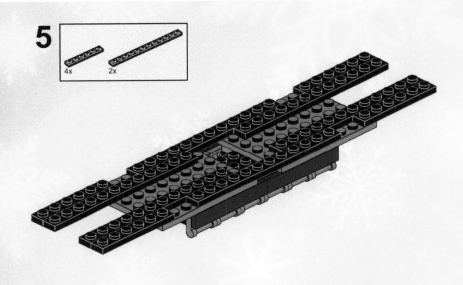

6

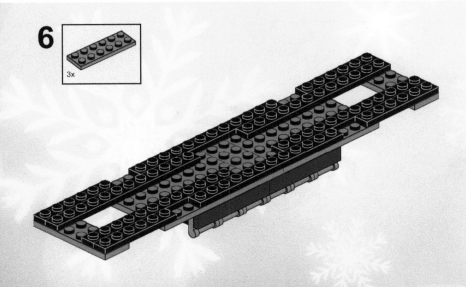

7

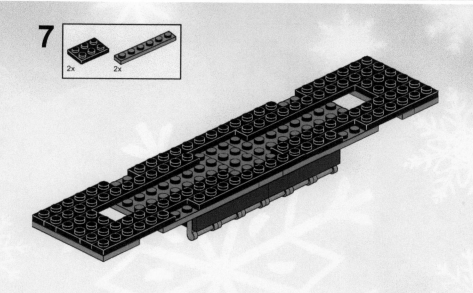

8

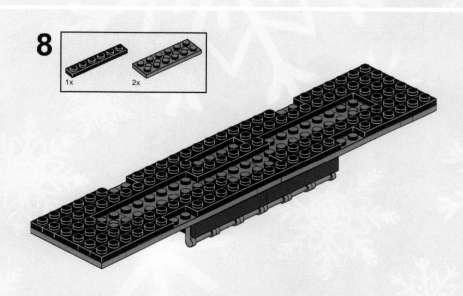

9

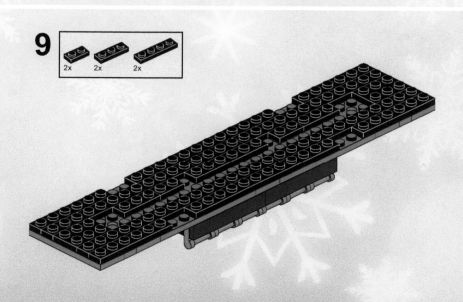

10

1x   2x

11

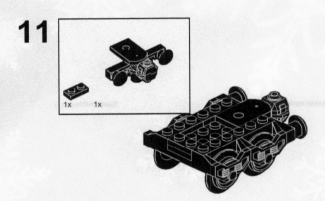

1x   1x

12

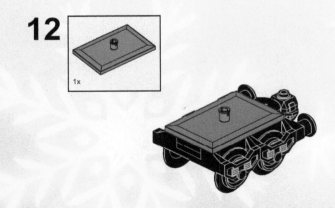

1x

13

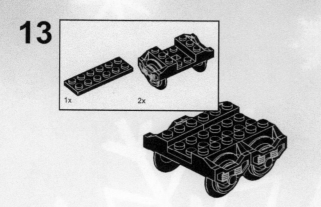

1x   2x

14

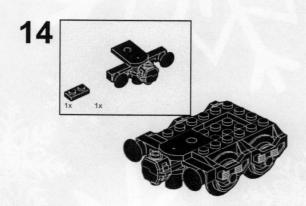

1x   1x

15

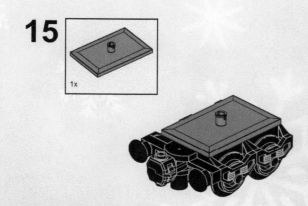

1x

16

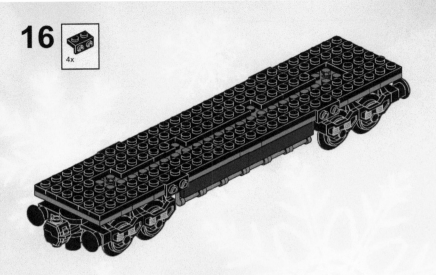

17

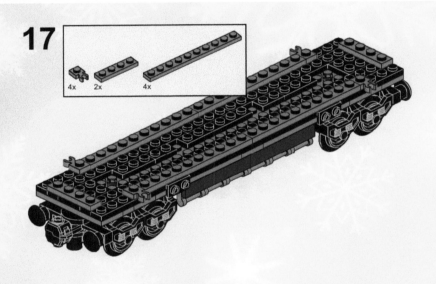

18

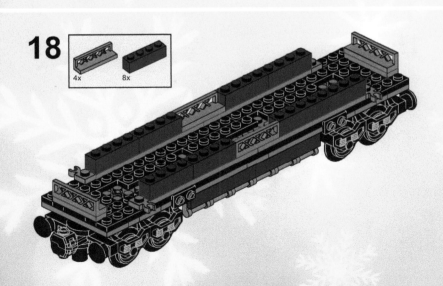

19

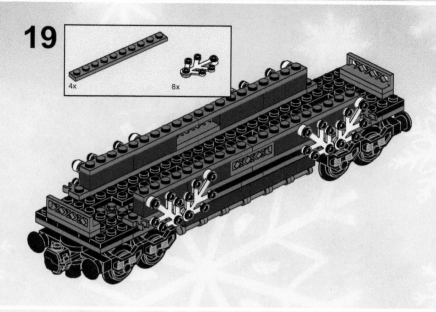

4x 8x

20

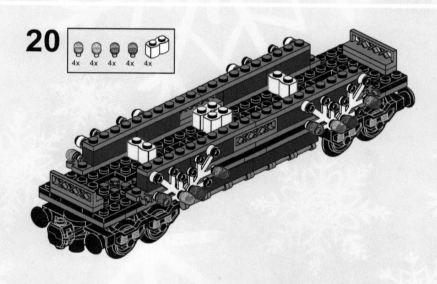

4x 4x 4x 4x 4x

21

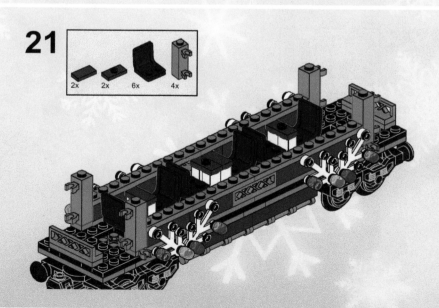

2x 2x 6x 4x

22

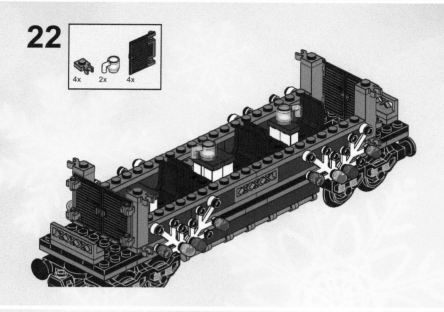

23

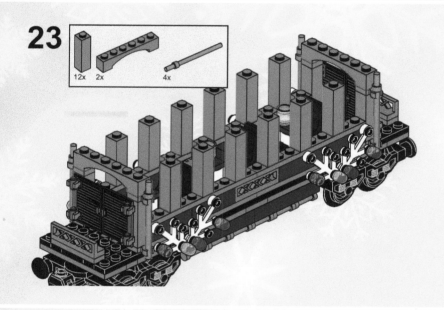

24

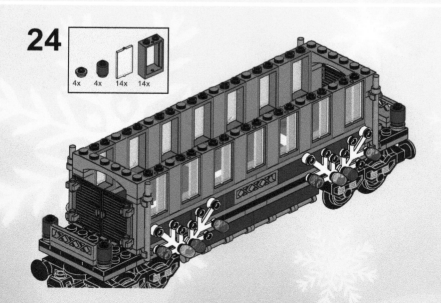

25

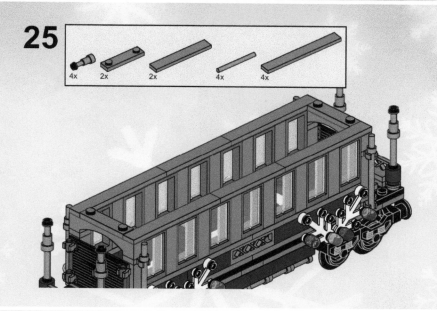

4x 2x 2x 4x 4x

26

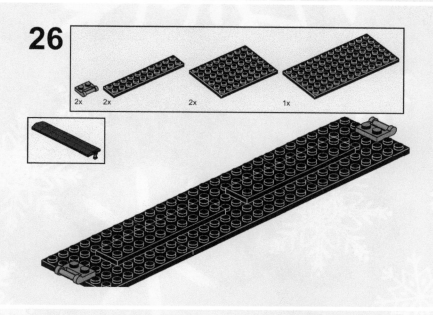

2x 2x 2x 1x

27

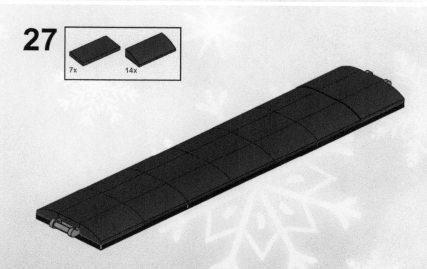

7x 14x

28

2x 2x 2x

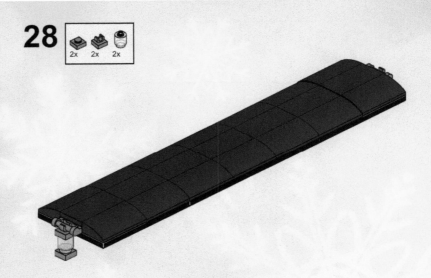

29

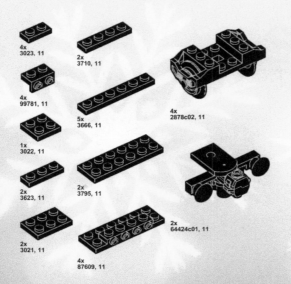

4x
3023, 11

2x
3710, 11

4x
99781, 11

5x
3666, 11

4x
2878c02, 11

1x
3022, 11

2x
3623, 11

2x
3795, 11

2x
64424c01, 11

2x
3021, 11

4x
87609, 11

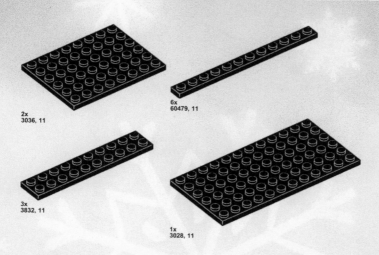

2x
3036, 11

6x
60479, 11

3x
3832, 11

1x
3028, 11

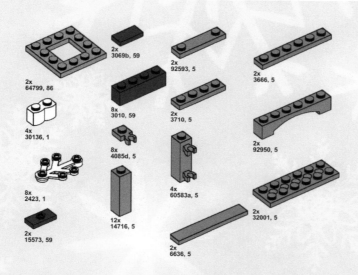

2x
64799, 86

2x
3069b, 59

2x
92593, 5

2x
3666, 5

4x
30136, 1

8x
3010, 59

2x
3710, 5

8x
4085d, 5

2x
92950, 5

8x
2423, 1

4x
60583a, 5

2x
32001, 5

2x
15573, 59

12x
14716, 5

2x
6636, 5

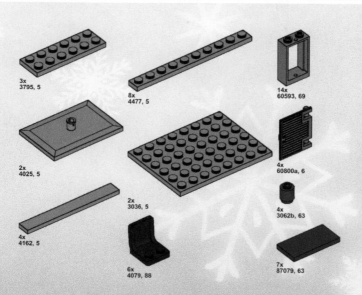

3x
3795, 5

8x
4477, 5

14x
60593, 69

2x
4025, 5

4x
60800a, 6

4x
4162, 5

2x
3036, 5

4x
3062b, 63

6x
4079, 88

7x
87079, 63

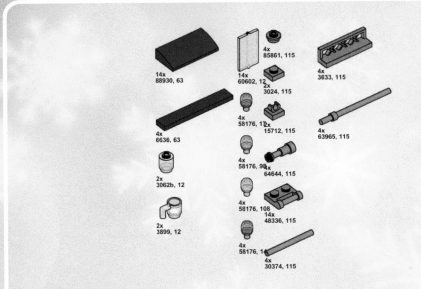

14x
88930, 63

14x
60602, 12

4x
85861, 115

2x
3024, 115

4x
3633, 115

4x
6636, 63

4x
58176, 12

2x
15712, 115

4x
63965, 115

2x
3062b, 12

4x
58176, 98

4x
64644, 115

2x
3899, 12

4x
58176, 108

14x
48336, 115

4x
58176, 14

4x
30374, 115

HOT COCOA TANKER

Number of bricks: 204

www.inklingbricks.com/parts/hotcocoatanker.txt

1

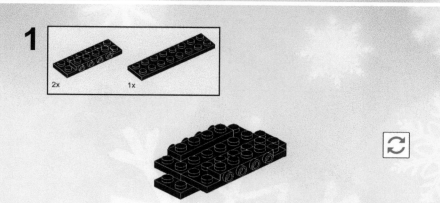

2

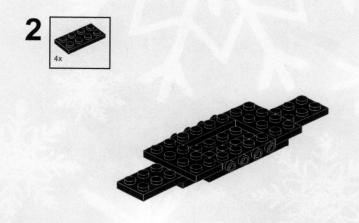

3

4

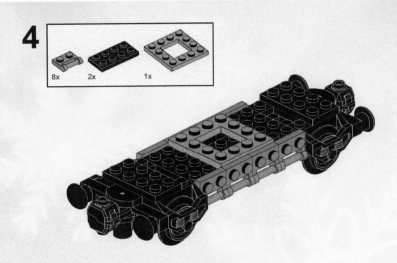

8x 2x 1x

5

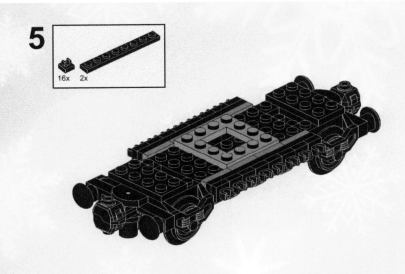

16x 2x

6

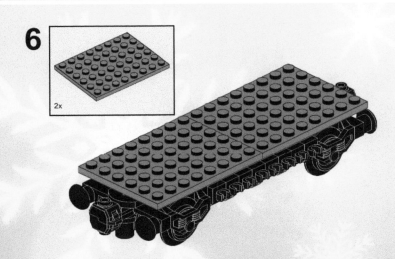

2x

7

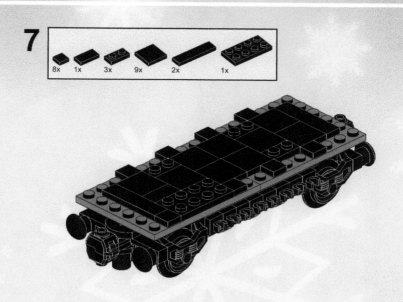

8x 1x 3x 9x 2x 1x

8

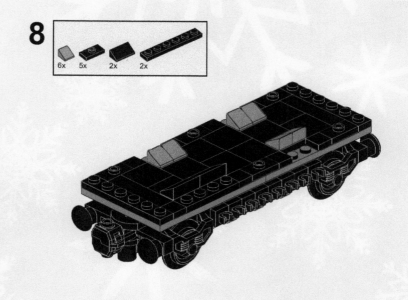

6x 5x 2x 2x

9

2x 2x 1x 1x

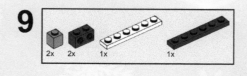

10

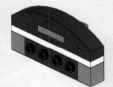

11

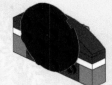

12

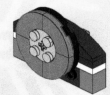

13

2x

14

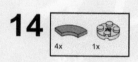

4x   1x

15

1x   1x

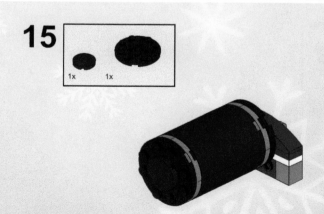

16

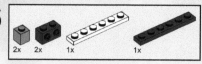

17

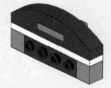

18

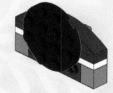

19

4x   1x

20

2x

21

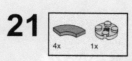

4x   1x

22

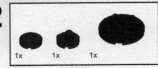

23

24

25

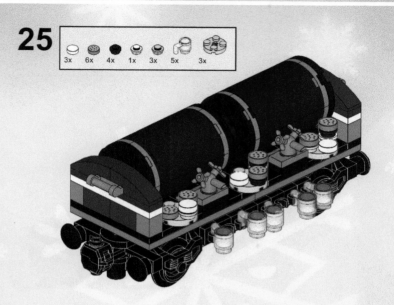

26

27

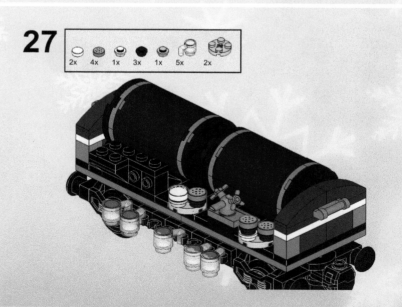

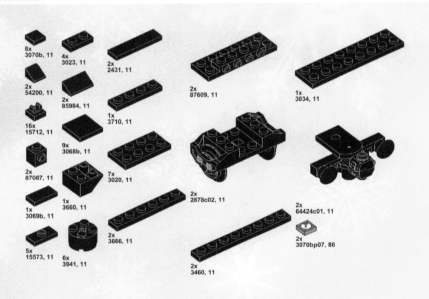

8x
3070b, 11

4x
3023, 11

2x
2431, 11

2x
87609, 11

1x
3034, 11

2x
54200, 11

2x
85984, 11

16x
15712, 11

1x
3710, 11

9x
3068b, 11

7x
3020, 11

87087, 11
2x

1x
3069b, 11

1x
3660, 11

2x
2878c02, 11

2x
64424c01, 11

5x
15573, 11

6x
3941, 11

2x
3666, 11

2x
3460, 11

2x
3070bp07, 86

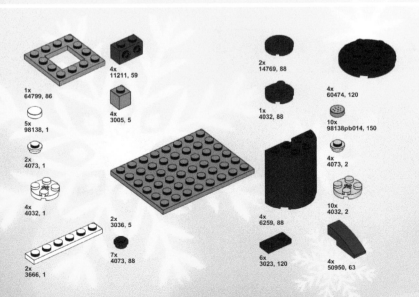

1x
64799, 86

4x
11211, 59

2x
14769, 88

4x
60474, 120

5x
98138, 1

4x
3005, 5

1x
4032, 88

10x
98138pb014, 150

2x
4073, 1

4x
4073, 2

4x
4032, 1

2x
3036, 5

4x
6259, 88

10x
4032, 2

2x
3666, 1

7x
4073, 88

6x
3023, 120

4x
50950, 63

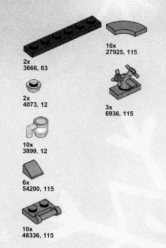

2x
3666, 63

16x
27925, 115

2x
4073, 12

3x
6936, 115

10x
3899, 12

6x
54200, 115

10x
48336, 115

REINDEER CAR

Number of bricks: 123

www.inklingbricks.com/parts/reindeercar.txt

1

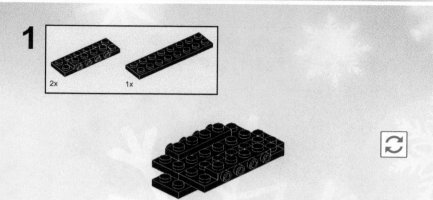

2x   1x

2

4x

3

2x   2x

4

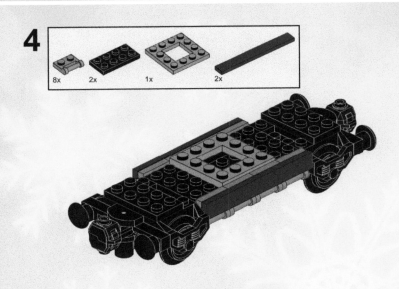

8x 2x 1x 2x

5

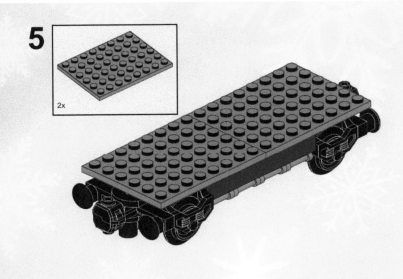

2x

6

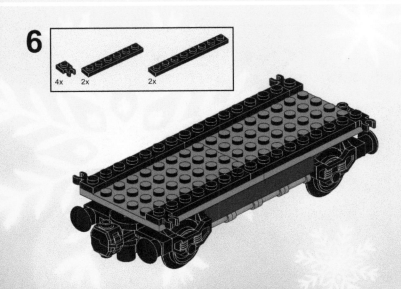

4x 2x 2x

7

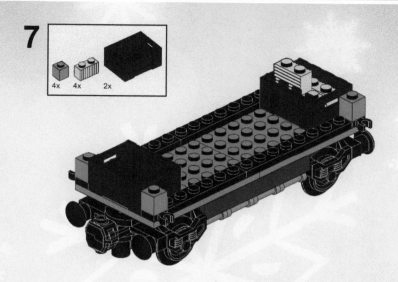

4x 4x 2x

8

4x 2x 2x

9

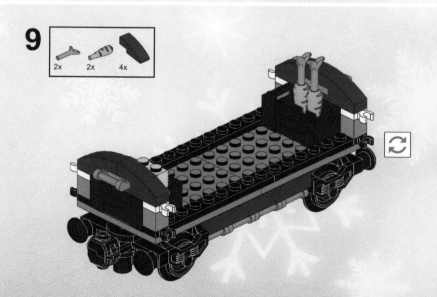

2x 2x 4x

10

11

8x

12

2x 1x

13

14

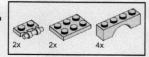

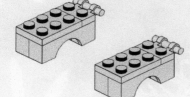

15

8x

16

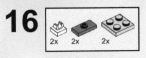

17

18

19

2x   4x   2x

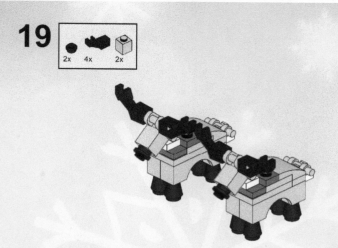

20

4x

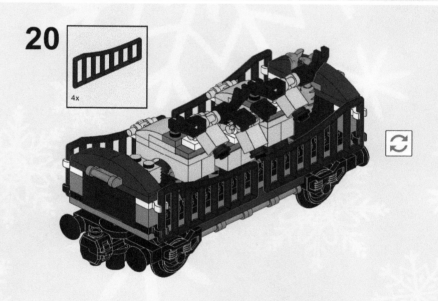

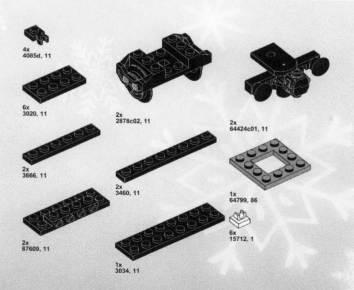

4x
4085d, 11

6x
3020, 11

2x
2878c02, 11

2x
64424c01, 11

2x
3666, 11

2x
3460, 11

1x
64799, 86

2x
87609, 11

1x
3034, 11

6x
15712, 1

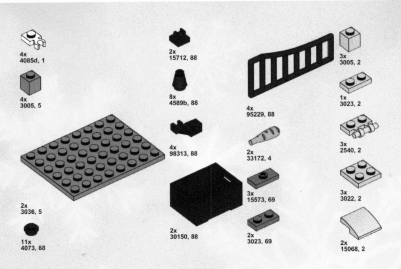

4x
4085d, 1

4x
3005, 5

2x
3036, 5

11x
4073, 88

2x
15712, 88

8x
4589b, 88

4x
98313, 88

2x
30150, 88

4x
95229, 88

2x
33172, 4

3x
15573, 69

2x
3023, 69

3x
3005, 2

1x
3023, 2

3x
2540, 2

3x
3022, 2

2x
15068, 2

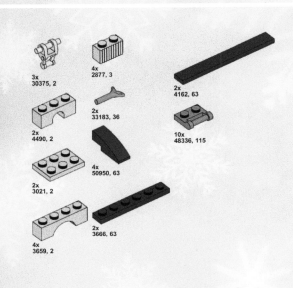

3x
30375, 2

2x
4490, 2

2x
3021, 2

4x
3659, 2

4x
2877, 3

2x
33183, 36

4x
50950, 63

2x
3666, 63

2x
4162, 63

10x
48336, 115

GINGERBREAD CAR

Number of bricks: 218

www.inklingbricks.com/parts/gingerbreadcar.txt

1

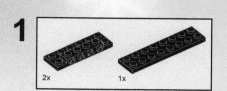

2x   1x

2

4x

3

2x   2x

4

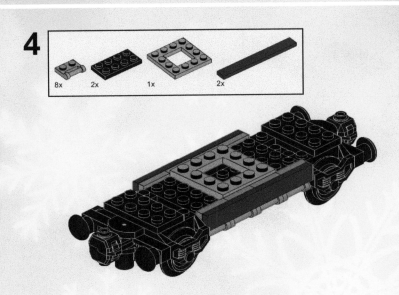

8x 2x 1x 2x

5

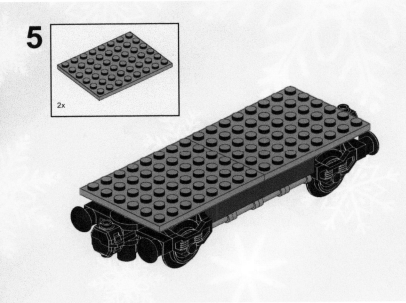

2x

6

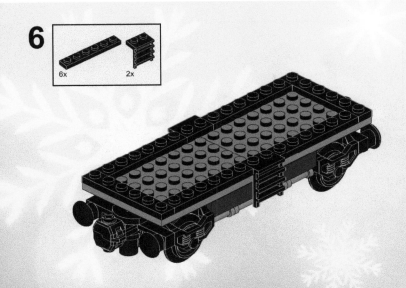

6x 2x

7

6x 2x 2x 2x 4x

8

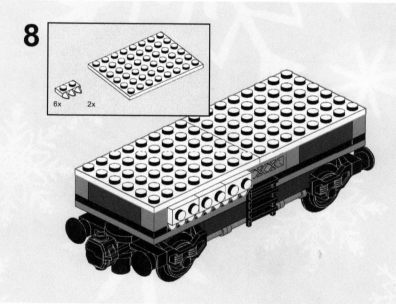

6x 2x

9

2x 2x 2x 3x

10

4x 4x 1x

11

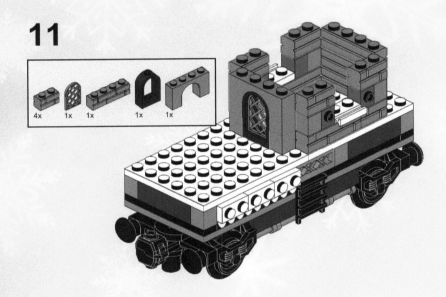

4x 1x 1x 1x 1x

12

4x 4x 4x 4x 12x

13

14

15

16

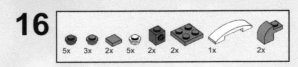

5x 3x 2x 5x 2x 2x 1x 2x

17

1x 1x 2x 1x 1x

18

1x 8x 2x 1x

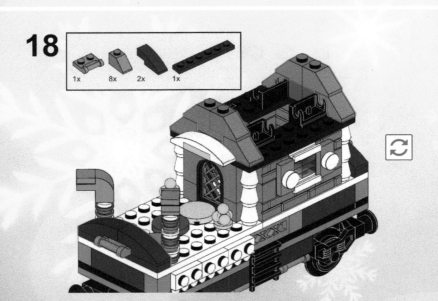

19

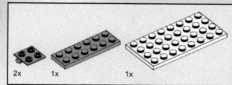

2x 1x 1x

20

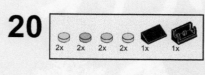

2x 2x 2x 2x 1x 1x

21

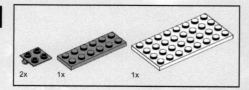

2x 1x 1x

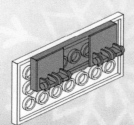

22

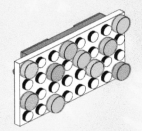

2x 3x 2x 3x

23

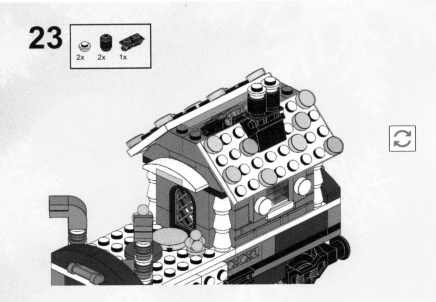

2x 2x 1x

24

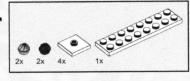

2x 2x 4x 1x

2x
3062b, 11

6x
3020, 11

1x
85984, 11

6x
3666, 11

5x
3937, 11

2x
2878c02, 11

2x
64424c01, 11

1x
3938, 11

2x
87609, 11

1x
3034, 11

2x
87087, 86

4x
6134, 86

2x
4175, 11

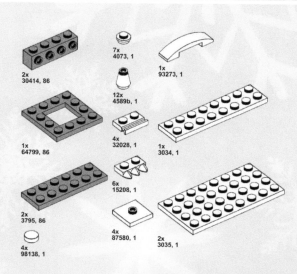

2x
30414, 86

7x
4073, 1

1x
93273, 1

12x
4589b, 1

1x
64799, 86

4x
32028, 1

1x
3034, 1

6x
15208, 1

2x
3795, 86

4x
98138, 1

4x
87580, 1

2x
3035, 1

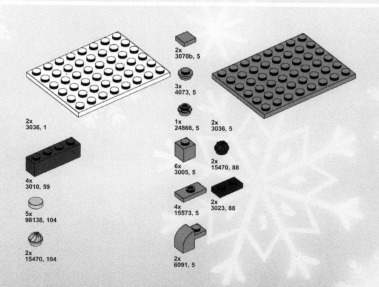

2x
3070b, 5

3x
4073, 5

2x
3036, 1

1x
24866, 5

2x
3036, 5

4x
3010, 59

6x
3005, 5

2x
15470, 88

5x
98138, 104

4x
15573, 5

2x
3023, 88

2x
15470, 104

2x
6091, 5

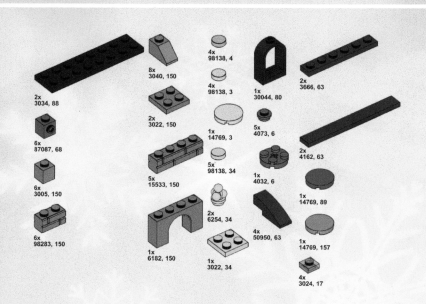

2x
3034, 88

8x
3040, 150

4x
98138, 4

1x
30044, 80

2x
3666, 63

6x
87087, 68

2x
3022, 150

4x
98138, 3

5x
4073, 6

6x
3005, 150

5x
15533, 150

1x
14769, 3

2x
4162, 63

5x
98138, 34

1x
4032, 6

6x
98283, 150

2x
6254, 34

1x
14769, 89

1x
6182, 150

4x
50950, 63

1x
3022, 34

1x
14769, 157

4x
3024, 17

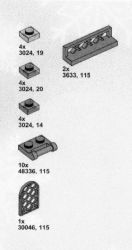

4x
3024, 19

2x
3633, 115

4x
3024, 20

4x
3024, 14

10x
48336, 115

1x
30046, 115

PRESENT CAR

Number of bricks: 268

www.inklingbricks.com/parts/presentcar.txt

1

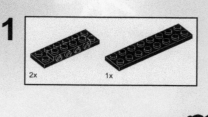

2x   1x

2

4x

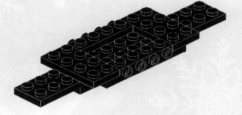

3

2x   2x

4

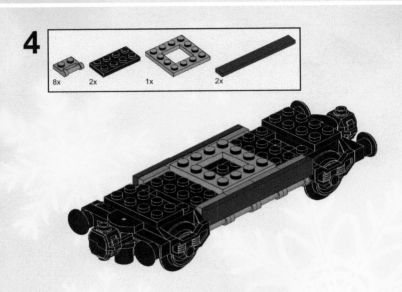

8x 2x 1x 2x

5

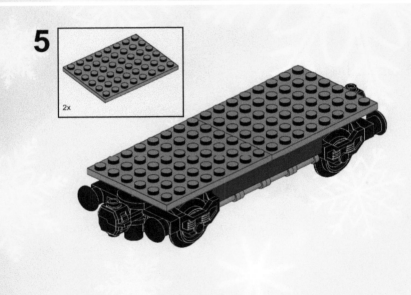

2x

6

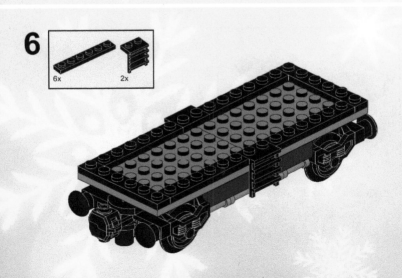

6x 2x

7

8

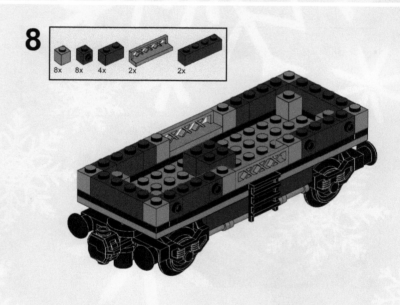

9

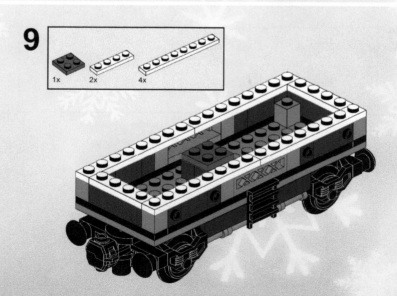

10

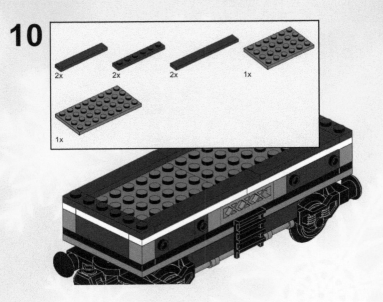

2x 2x 2x 1x

1x

11

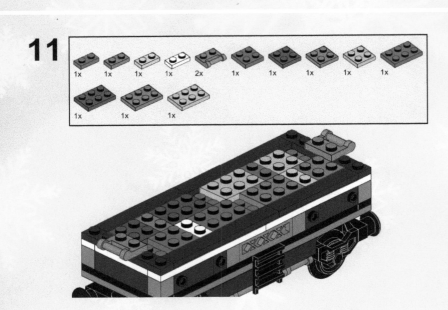

1x 1x 1x 1x 2x 1x 1x 1x 1x 1x

1x 1x 1x

12

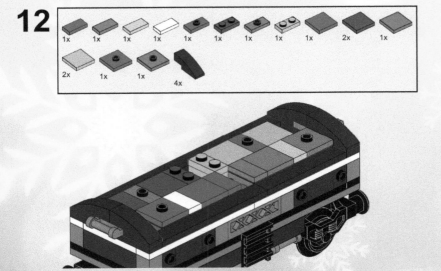

1x 1x 1x 1x 1x 1x 1x 1x 1x 2x 1x

2x 1x 1x 4x

13

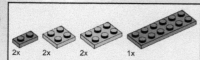

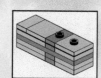

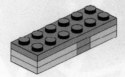

14

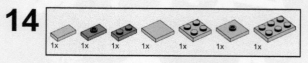

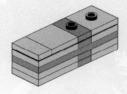

15

16

1x 2x 1x 1x 1x

17

3x 3x 6x 3x 3x 3x 3x 3x 3x

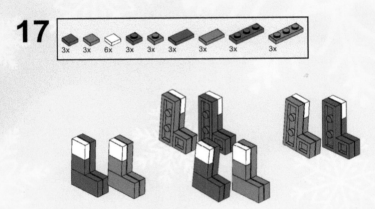

18

19

 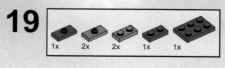

20

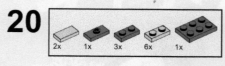

21

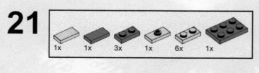

22

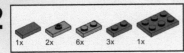 1x 2x 6x 3x 1x

23

24 1x 2x 1x

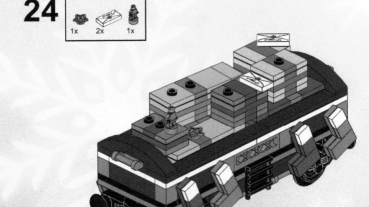

25

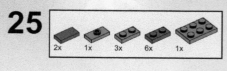

2x 1x 3x 6x 1x

26

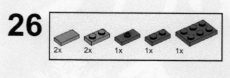

2x 2x 1x 1x 1x

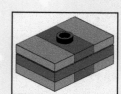

27

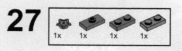

1x 1x 1x 1x

28

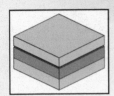

29

30

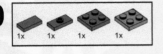

31

 2x  1x 1x 2x 1x

32

 1x 1x 1x 1x

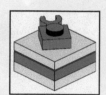

33

34

35

36

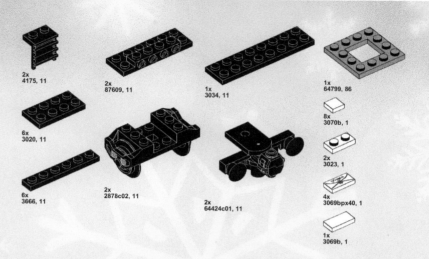

2x
4175, 11

2x
87609, 11

1x
3034, 11

1x
64799, 86

6x
3020, 11

2x
2878c02, 11

2x
64424c01, 11

8x
3070b, 1

2x
3023, 1

4x
3069bpx40, 1

1x
3069b, 1

6x
3666, 11

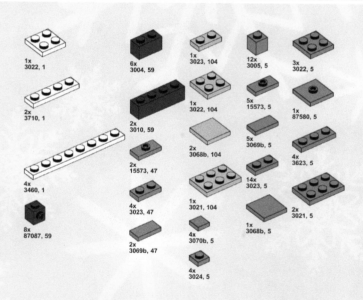

1x
3022, 1

2x
3710, 1

4x
3460, 1

8x
87087, 59

6x
3004, 59

2x
3010, 59

2x
15573, 47

4x
3023, 47

2x
3069b, 47

1x
3023, 104

1x
3022, 104

2x
3068b, 104

1x
3021, 104

4x
3070b, 5

4x
3024, 5

12x
3005, 5

5x
15573, 5

5x
3069b, 5

14x
3023, 5

1x
3068b, 5

3x
3022, 5

1x
87580, 5

4x
3623, 5

2x
3021, 5

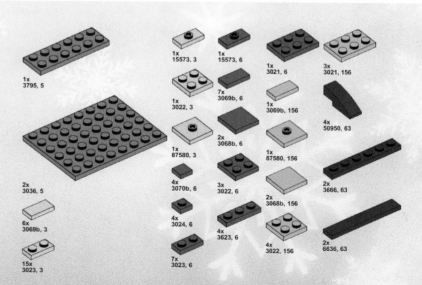

1x
3795, 5

2x
3036, 5

6x
3069b, 3

15x
3023, 3

1x
15573, 3

1x
3022, 3

1x
87580, 3

4x
3070b, 6

4x
3024, 6

7x
3023, 6

1x
15573, 6

7x
3069b, 6

2x
3068b, 6

3x
3022, 6

4x
3623, 6

1x
3021, 6

1x
3069b, 156

1x
87580, 156

2x
3068b, 156

4x
3022, 156

3x
3021, 156

4x
50950, 63

2x
3666, 63

2x
6636, 63

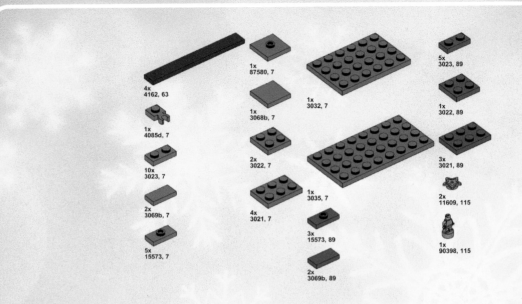

4x
4162, 63

1x
4085d, 7

10x
3023, 7

2x
3069b, 7

5x
15573, 7

1x
87580, 7

1x
3068b, 7

2x
3022, 7

4x
3021, 7

1x
3035, 7

3x
15573, 89

2x
3069b, 89

1x
3032, 7

5x
3023, 89

1x
3022, 89

3x
3021, 89

2x
11609, 115

1x
90398, 115

10x
48336, 115

2x
3633, 115

TREE CAR

Number of bricks: 117

www.inklingbricks.com/parts/treecar.txt

1

2x 1x

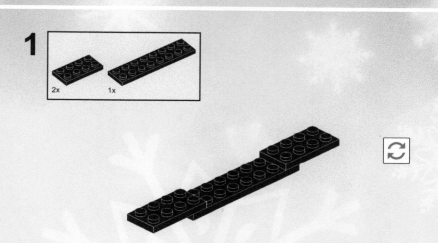

2

2x

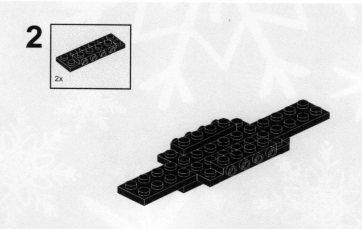

3

2x

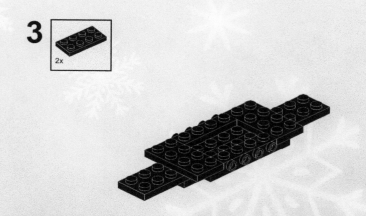

4

2x

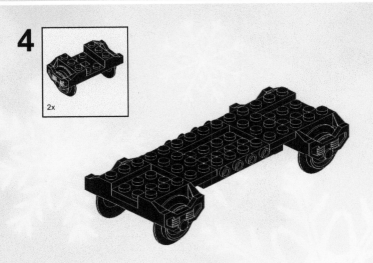

5

8x   2x

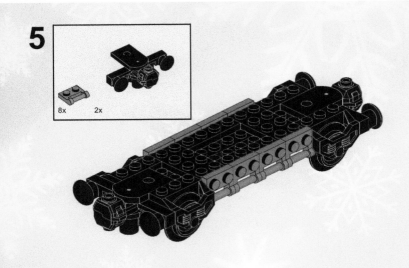

6

2x   1x   2x

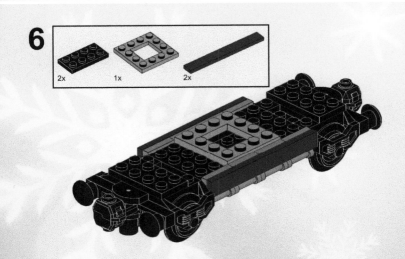

7

2x

8

8x 2x

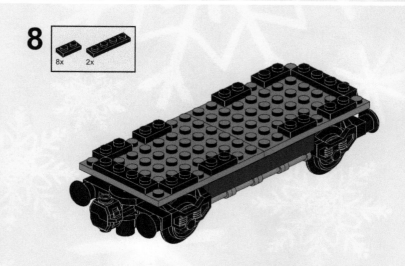

9

12x

10

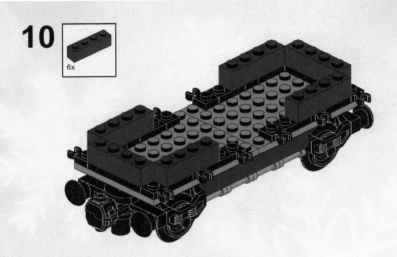

11

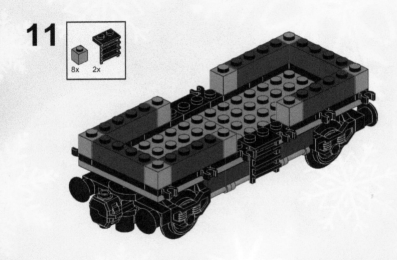

12

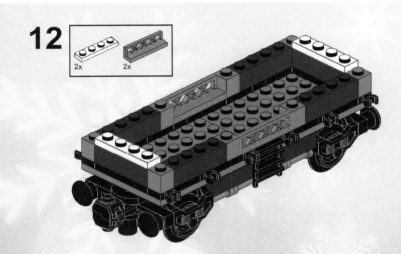

13

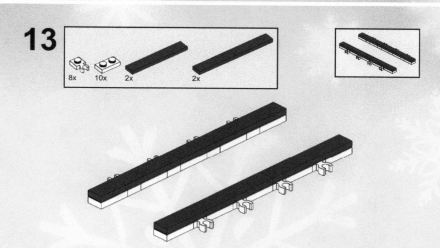

14

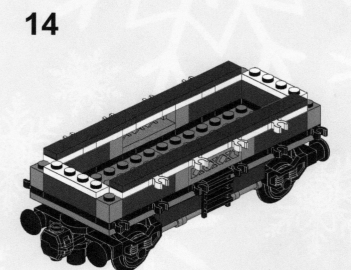

15

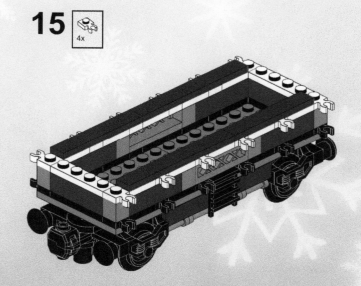

16

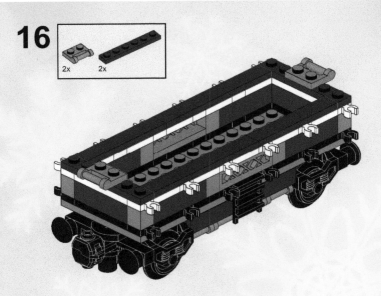

17

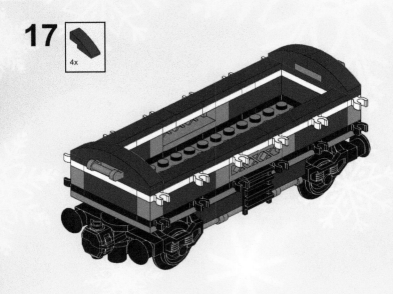

18

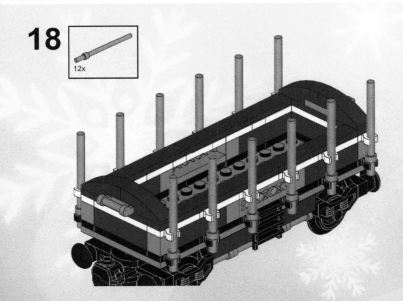

19

3x

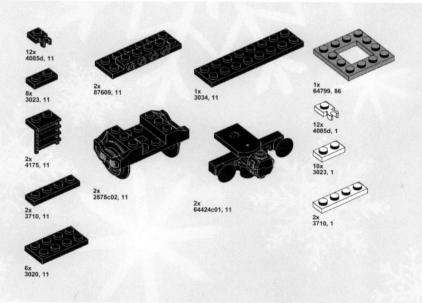

12x
4085d, 11

8x
3023, 11

2x
87609, 11

1x
3034, 11

1x
64799, 86

2x
4175, 11

2x
2878c02, 11

2x
64424c01, 11

12x
4085d, 1

10x
3023, 1

2x
3710, 11

2x
3710, 1

6x
3020, 11

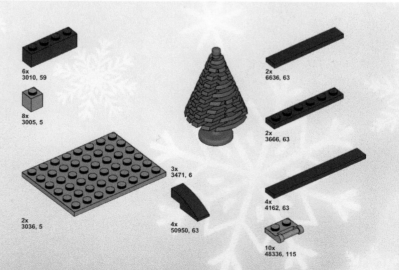

6x
3010, 59

8x
3005, 5

3x
3471, 6

2x
6636, 63

2x
3666, 63

2x
3036, 5

4x
50950, 63

4x
4162, 63

10x
48336, 115

2x
3633, 115

12x
63965, 115

COLLECT THE FULL SERIES!

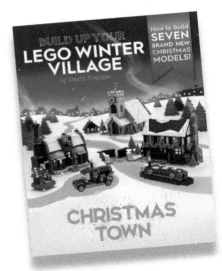

CHRISTMAS TOWN

CHRISTMAS TRAIN

CHRISTMAS TRAIN 2

CHRISTMAS MOUNTAIN

CHRISTMAS FAIR

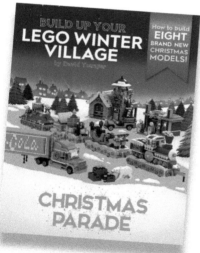

CHRISTMAS PARADE

CHRISTMAS STORIES

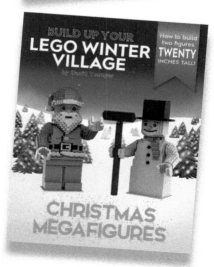

CHRISTMAS MEGAFIGURES

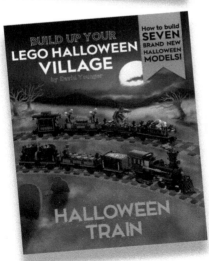

HALLOWEEN TRAIN

Available at www.inklingbricks.com

Printed in the USA
CPSIA information can be obtained
at www.ICGtesting.com
LVHW071241171023
761168LV00034B/648